PUZZLE POPPERS

BY GERARD MOSLER

Illustrated by Tad Krumeich

SCHOLASTIC INC.
New York Toronto London Auckland Sydney

ISBN 0-590-10275-3

12 11 10 9 8 7 6 5 4 3 2 1   0 1 2 3 4 5/9

Printed in the U.S.A.

23

EXPLOSIVE CROSSWORD

All the words of this puzzle have a thing in common.
Can you guess what it is?

Across
2. Ice treat.
4. Kind of art or music.
5. Well liked.
7. A toy gun is a _____.
10. Kind of flower.

Down
1. "_____ goes the weasel."
2. Roasted kernels.
3. Kind of drink (2 words).
6. Hero of cartoons.
8. Boston summer concerts.
9. Close relative (slang).

BIG DAY

It started in '76 but it's a big day every year! Each of the sentences below contains three letters of this day. Underline those letters, put them in the boxes below, and presto! Big day!

1. "... Wearin' out your grinders, eatin' goober peas."
2. Cortez could have used a good insect repellent.
3. A blunderbuss was an old gun, not a clumsy bus.
4. There'll be commencement exercises when you graduate.
5. This national holiday has a fixed date.

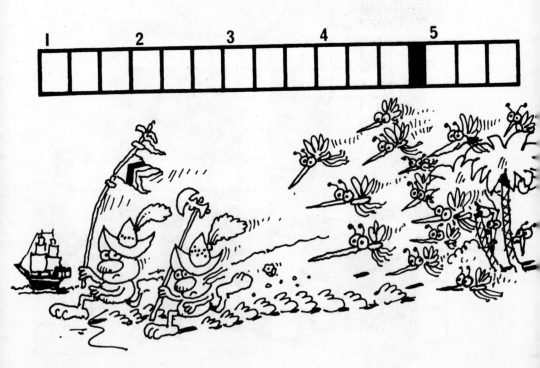

MAGIC SQUARES

Find a relative who takes a part of everybody's money.

1. Your mother's or father's brother to you.
2. Roman emperor who liked fires; also _____ Wolfe.
3. High, rocky bluffs.
4. Cut tree trunk or limb.
5. Fifth letter of alphabet.
6. Nickname for Samuel.

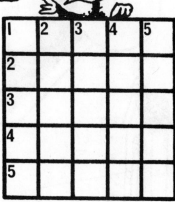

Use the clues to reveal a big bird.

1. Rip in clothes (with "a").
2. To annoy, for fun.
3. The big bird.
4. Used for coasting (with "a").
5. Tall grass growing in shallow water.

MOVING THE SENTRIES

Four sentries are on guard at points A, C, D, and E. Put two nickels on spaces A and E to represent privates. Put two dimes on spaces C and D for two sergeants. Now, making one move at a time along the tracks shown, reverse the positions of the sergeants (dimes) and the privates (nickels) in the shortest number of moves.

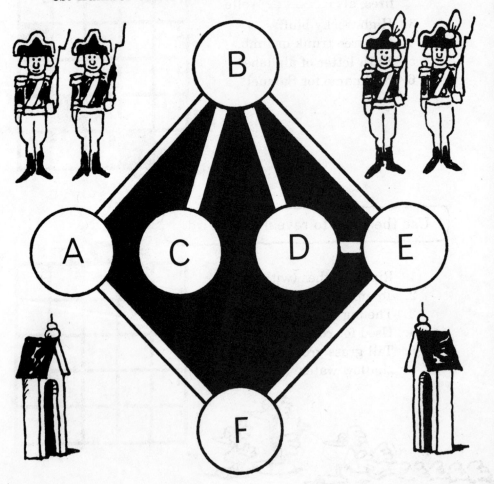

PICK YOUR COLORS

Everyone knows the colors of the flag. Or do they?
Here's a list of fancy names for plain old red, white,
and blue. Can you spot the color each stands for?

_____ 1. SAPPHIRE	_____13. POPPY
_____ 2. AUBURN	_____14. ROUGE
_____ 3. CHALKY	_____15. RUBY
_____ 4. CHERRY	_____16. SCARLET
_____ 5. CRIMSON	_____17. SKY
_____ 6. BEET	_____18. SNOWY
_____ 7. AQUA	_____19. TOMATO
_____ 8. FLAME	_____20. PEARL
_____ 9. LOBSTER	_____21. RASPBERRY
_____10. MARINE	_____22. MIDNIGHT
_____11. MILKY	_____23. LILY (Easter)
_____12. NAVY	_____24. STRAWBERRY

WORDS FROM THE WHITE HOUSE

How many words of two or more letters can you find in the White House? Start at any letter and go to any letter next to it in any direction. In this puzzle, you do not have to go in a straight line. For example, you can go from O to U to T. You can use a letter twice in a word, but you must move each time and you cannot skip over letters. Abbreviations are also okay if you find any. Over twenty words is a good score.

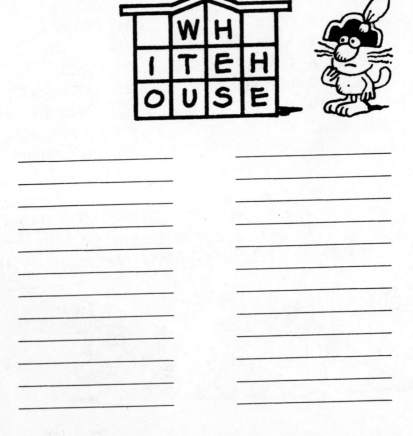

_____   _____
_____   _____
_____   _____
_____   _____
_____   _____
_____   _____
_____   _____
_____   _____
_____   _____

DISCOVERY ACROSTIC

How did Columbus know the world was round?
The answer to this riddle will appear in the boxes below. Just fill in the spaces beside each clue and put the numbered letters in the right boxes.

A. To clean or dry __ __ __ __
  3   10

B. To aid   __ __ __ __
  1 4

C. To tie securely __ __ __ __
  5 8 6

D. To hold out (endure) __ __ __ __
  7

E. To make less __ __ __ __ __ __
  2 9 11

1	2	3	4	5	6	7	8	9	10	11

SEAT A TREASURED MAN

Seat one of Washington's most trusted cabinet members by placing these letters in this order:
Put T opposite A, which is on the left of M and to the right of H. T is to the left of L, between L and O. N is opposite I, which is between M and L.

PRESIDENTIAL PATTER

From the names of the Presidents below, pick the PUNNY (not factual) answers to these questions:

1. Which Presidents had land? _____
2. Who always let people
   have their way?   _____
3. Who was the sharpest?   _____
4. Who was the slowest?   _____
5. Who was a dentist?   _____
6. Who had "real cool"?   _____
7. Who was well connected?   _____
8. How many were sons? _____

PIERCE	GRANT	CLEVELAND	MADISON
COOLIDGE	GARFIELD	WILSON	POLK
LINCOLN	JEFFERSON	FILLMORE	JACKSON
HARRISON	JOHNSON	HOOVER	TRUMAN
KENNEDY	NIXON	HAYES	TYLER

WHICH PRESIDENT'S NAME IS ALSO THAT OF A FAMOUS CAR..??..

STAR ATHLETES

Unscramble the names of the sports stars below, then find them in the word search puzzle.

Ice-Skating Stars: salnyron mursesn, nelaie ykaaz, roohydt malihl

Tennis Stars: jrobn robg, iarmtan ravnatiaovl

Basketball Stars: rameek dalub brbaja, yarlr ribd

Football Stars: oej thamna, eoj renge, rergo bhactuas

Track Stars: yarm kedcer, ynevle shadrof

Swimming Star: karm tipzs

Golf Stars: ele tronive, canny zepol

Baseball Stars: bbea thur, gioy raber

Gymnastics Stars: dania nocamiec, goal burokt

Hockey Stars: obb styromn, bybbo ror, yanew tregkyz

Boxing Stars: dammahum lai, eoj reizafr

Auto Racing Stars: ja yoft, la suner, rioam danterit

PET HATE CROSSWORD

Complete this crossword and you will spy a hated name among patriots in the American Revolution.

Across:

1. Long _____ (past).
4. Informal hello.
6. Ballpoint _____.
7. "___ Little Indians."
8. _____ and fro.
9. Dracula's pet.
10. Not gentle.
12. Weapon.
13. One in 7 down.
15. Fish or hair _____.
16. Professional (abbrev.).
17. American Telegraph (abbrev.).
18. Fuss or trouble (old-fashioned word).

Down:

1. Skillful.
2. Mystery name.
3. Put the silver _____ the table.
4. Mystery name continued.
5. "Go _____ and out the window."
7. Chasing game.
9. Roll (bread).
11. In and _____.
14. _____ many jobs for one.
15. North America (abbrev.)
16. Father, for short.

STAR DIVIDER

Can you draw two squares and two triangles so that every star is separated from every other one?

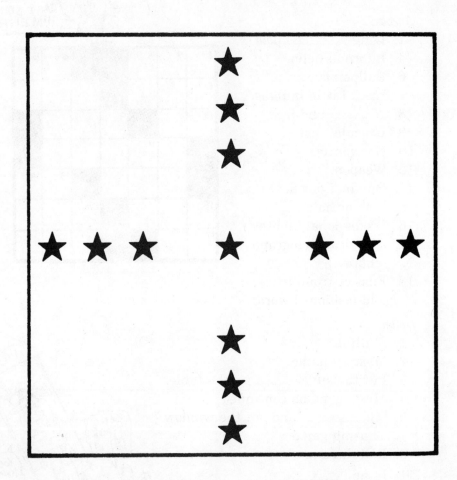

LADIES' MATCH

From the names below, can you choose the first ladies who fit these facts?

1. A great hostess, for whom an ice cream brand is named. _____

2. She was young, beautiful, and wore Paris clothes. _____

3. An ugly duckling, she became a world traveler, great humanitarian, and was a UN delegate. _____

4. The first, first lady. _____

5. She was first lady during the Civil War. _____

6. She was the wife of one President and mother of another. _____

MAMIE EISENHOWER ABIGAIL ADAMS
MARTHA WASHINGTON JACQUELINE KENNEDY
BESS TRUMAN ELEANOR ROOSEVELT
MARY LINCOLN GRACE COOLIDGE
DOLLY MADISON PATRICIA NIXON

POLITICS PATTER

Why is a vote in Congress like a bad cold?

Because sometimes the ayes (eyes) have it, and sometimes the noes.

Why are many politicians like lobsters?

Because they change color when they get into hot water.

At some political parties what game might be played?

Pin the tail on the donkey.

What causes political undercurrents in our nation's capital?

It's in D.C., isn't it?

FAMOUS FIRSTS

1. What tradition did Washington start that all Presidents up to F.D.R. observed?

   _____ TERMS _____   _____

2. Who began the tradition of the President opening the baseball season by tossing the first ball?

   W _____ H. T _____

3. Who was the first (and is still our only) bachelor President?

   J _____ B _____

4. Who created the first national parks?

   T _____ R _____

5. Who was the first President to occupy the White House?

   J_____ A _____

6. Who was the first President to visit Communist China?

   R _____ M. N _____

7. A "doll" of a hostess, this first lady started the Easter tradition of egg-rolling on the White House lawn.

   D _____ M _____

CONSTITUTIONAL

How's your constitution? In this puzzle the Constitution forms the backbone of twelve short words. Can you guess them from the clues?

1. ___ CN ___   Outdoor party.
2. ___ OO ___   Almost now.
3. ___ NI ___   To weave with two long needles.
4. ___ ST ___   Thick stuff for gluing.
5. ___ TU ___   Don't _____ your toe.
6. ___ IT ___   Nip.
7. ___ TI ___   To mix.
8. ___ UT ___   Soundless.
9. ___ TS ___   You put this on your hamburger.
10. ___ IN ___   To press hard with thumb and forefinger.
11. ___ OO ___   Not cold but _____.
12. ___ NC ___   Come at _____

COAST GUARD PATROL

There's been some smuggling by small sailing craft carrying sails marked like those below. As a Coast Guard officer you must know these designs so well you can redraw them. Study them carefully, then try to draw them on the blank sails on the next page.

PRESIDENTS IN HIDING

Thirteen Presidents are hiding in these sentences. Underline them as you find them.

1. Answer the question with a 'yes' or 'no.'
2. "Make the attic level and straight," the builder told the contractor.
3. The beavers built a dam straight across the brook.
4. The old-style reading lamp is worth a fortune.
5. Near the airplane hangar, fields of corn were ripening.
6. It's raining. Wear a poncho over your sweater.
7. "Get after him," screamed the store owner, who had been robbed.
8. Do you want to know what made John so nosy?
9. We must ask that Rumanian representative to attend the conference.
10. Who can afford to buy steak these days?
11. The big dog ran to his master.
12. Interpol knew all along that the leader of the crime organization was Higgins.
13. When Jacob's mad is on, keep away.

FAMOUS MONOGRAMS

Each of these portraits is entirely made up of letters. One spells out the name of a famous signer of the Declaration of Independence The other is a President. Can you name them?

BIRDS OF AMERICA WORD FIND

Can you find 26 birds in the puzzle below? Here are their names: BOBWHITE, EAGLE, CROW, TURKEY, WREN, SWALLOW, PHOEBE, FINCH, CRANE, CATBIRD, WARBLER, OWL, SPARROW, BLUEJAY, HAWK, QUAIL, ORIOLE, DUCK, GULL, THRUSH, CARDINAL, PIGEON, ROBIN, TERN, DOVE, SANDPIPER.

Draw a loop around the words as you find them.

TARGET PRACTICE

The early settlers had to keep up their hunting skills. They would hold target practice — to develop steadiness of hand and eye. How good is *your* eye? Can you tell which of these arrows are headed for the bull's eye?

MYSTERY LETTERS PUZZLE

All the words in this puzzle share two important letters.
Here are the clues:

1. Opposite of not good for anything.
2. Where you go to see paintings or relics.
3. Your uncle's son is your _____.
4. What you need when you stay out of school.
5. Where people and animals perform tricks.

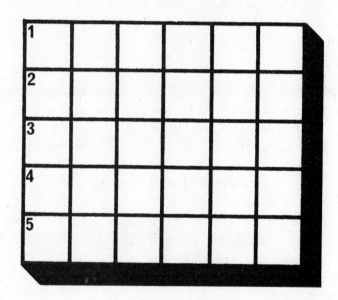

MONSTER NUMBER

7 0 1 3 5 0 1 0 0 1 7 7 6 1 9 7 6 1 8 6 5 2 4 1 0 0 1 6 2 0 1 0 9 0

What is it? Distance in light years to a quazar? The national debt? No, just the answers in a row to the puzzle opposite. Can you sort out the numbers, using the clues?

Across:
1. Number of original states in America.
2. Year of the Declaration of Independence.
4. Amount of the dollar bill that shows Franklin's portrait.
5. Amount that Peter Minuit paid the Indians for Manhattan Island.
6. Numbers in date of 1 down added together, times 10.
7. Number of original amendments in the Bill of Rights.
8. Number of stars in our flag.

Down:
1. Year the pilgrims landed at Plymouth.
2. Number of senators in the U.S. Senate.
3. Last two numbers of year of California Gold Rush added to 21.
4. American Bicentennial year.
7. Year the Civil War ended.

SWITCHES

Which state can be turned into a moneymaking scheme for the government just by switching 2 letters?

What word in the United States means exactly the opposite when two of its letters are switched?

What President's name can be turned into abbreviations (old) for two states?

What New England town is made up of males?

WHICH WITCH IS WATCHING WITCHES WATCHING A WITCH WATCH...??

← WITCH WATCH

FIREWORKS FOR THE FOURTH

Can you get WORK out of FIRE to make a fireworks display?

```
F   I   R   E
—   —   —   —

—   —   —   —
W   O   R   K
```

Here's a harder one. Can you turn FOUR into JULY to make a Four(th of) July celebration?

```
F   O   U   R
—   —   —   —

—   —   —   —

—   —   —   —
P   O   L   L
—   —   —   —

—   —   —   —
D   U   L   Y
J   U   L   Y
```

MYSTERY MAN OF HISTORY

He was a printer, inventor, statesman, writer, and one of our favorite founding fathers. If you can guess his name, fill in 2 down and 5 across. The rest is easy.

Across:
3. One of his famous sayings was: "Remember that _____ is money."
5. The mystery man's last name.
7. A stove named after him is a fireplace completely made of the metal _____.
8. Another of his sayings was: "God helps them that _____ themselves."
10. In his most famous experiment he flew a _____ with a key attached in a thunderstorm to prove that lightning is electricity.
11. He then invented the lightning _____.
12. One of his proverbs: "Little strokes fell great _____."

Down:
1. Mouth organ. (He invented it.)
2. First name of mystery man.
4. "Early to bed and early to rise, makes a _____ healthy, wealthy, and wise."
6. "Eat to live, and not _____ to eat."
9. Most of these sayings came from _____ *Richard's Almanac,* which he wrote and printed.

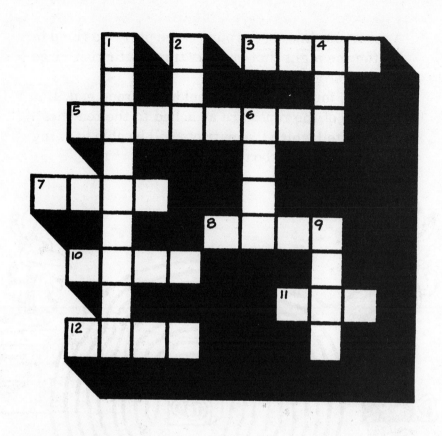

BIG TEA PARTY

As everyone knows, the biggest tea party was held in Boston the night that patriots threw a British cargo of tea overboard.

Below, four patriots are holding a rope end. But only two of the ropes are attached to the tea chest. Can you tell which two patriots will be able to swing this tea chest overboard?

PUT THE TEA BACK!

Instead of throwing the tea into the sea, the patriots might have used it in a puzzle like this. Put T E A in the right spaces to revive the "skeleton" words below. For example, add T E A to M—S——R and get MASTER.

1. S__ __ __ M
2. T R __ __ __
3. S __ __ __ S
4. W __ I __ __ R
5. L __ __ __
6. __ __ M __
7. __ __ S __
8. B __ __ S __

9. __ R __ __ D
10. D __ __ __ __ H
11. P L __ __ __
12. M __ __ __
13. S __ __ R __
14. P __ S __ __ __
15. M __ __ __ L
16. S __ __ K __

33

CLOTHING STATES

Q: If Florida and Virginia Con(n). Louisiana for Dakota Missouri, will Delaware New Jersey?
A: Idaho. Alaska.

Q: Did Minnesota New Jersey for Me.?
A: If So., Carolina, Iowa.

Q: Kentucky, did you So. Dakota Mississippi?
A: No, Dakota Georgia. Arkansas, too.

(Give up? Translation in answer section.)

MYSTERY LANDMARK

If you fill in the crossword using these clues you will
discover a famous place of Revolutionary times.

Across:
1. Place for baking or roasting.
5. Spoon for dipping out gravy.
6. Elevated (abbrev.).
7. Not young.
9. Bird of prey.
12. Prefix meaning water.
13. "The Bride___ Dracula."
14. Red Riding Hood met one.
17. Eggs of fish.
18. Another word for boast.
20. Flesh of animals.

Down:
1. Prefix of butter substitute.
2. The mystery place.
3. Man's nickname.
4. National League (abbrev.).
8. Short for father.
10. Great (abbrev.).
11. Word meaning behold.
12. _____ many pets
    do you have?
15. Same as 11 down.
16. What you walk on (plural).
19. After midnight (abbrev.).

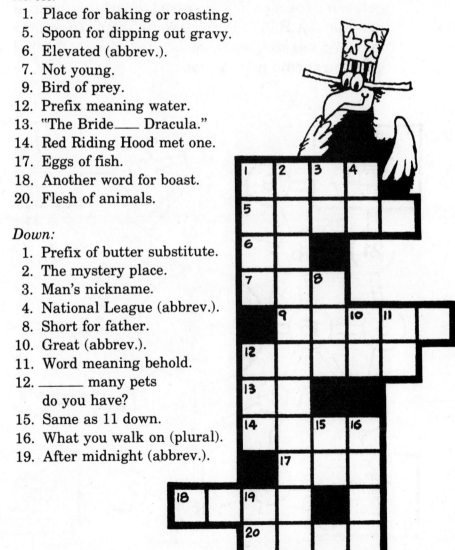

MILITARY MAZE

During the Revolution a Connecticut officer was ordered to collect 100 men from various towns. (Circles on maze show numbers of waiting men.) After gathering the men he was to lead them to the nearest garrison—A,B,C, or D. What route should the officer take to get exactly 100 men as fast as possible? What garrison should he head for?

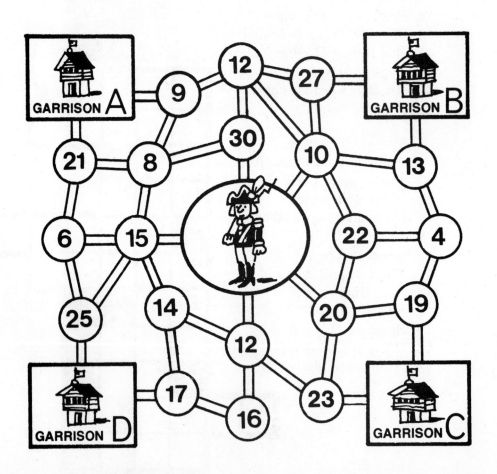

WHO SAID IT?

From the names below can you pick the President who said this:

1. "A house divided against itself cannot stand."

   _____

2. "Speak softly but carry a big stick."

   _____

3. "The world must be made safe for democracy."

   _____

4. "Prosperity is just around the corner."

   _____

5. "The only thing we have to fear is fear itself."

   _____

6. "The buck stops here."

   _____

7. "Ask not what your country can do for you—ask what you can do for your country."

   _____

T. ROOSEVELT	H. HOOVER
H. S. TRUMAN	A. LINCOLN
J. F. KENNEDY	F. D. ROOSEVELT
W. WILSON	A. JACKSON

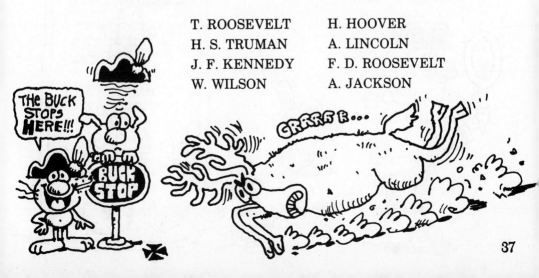

Between these rows of letters lies a secret word that was a reason for the colonists to fight the Revolution. To find the secret word fill in the blanks with letters that will make words. One is completed as an example.

```
P  O  A  T  A  S  I  A  B  E  I  W
I  _  _  _  _  _  _  _  _  _  _  _
E  E  E  A  E  N  D  E  D  E  E  E
```

FAMOUS INITIALS MATCH

Draw a line from initials to famous act. (Super if you can name the people too!)

N.H.

H.H.

P.R.

T.J.

W.B.

J.P.J.

W.P.

P.S.

J.S.

J.H.

B.R.

C.C.

a. Pilgrim governor of Plymouth Plantation

b. Quaker who founded Pennsylvania

c. American spy hanged by British

d. He rode to tell farmers, "The British are coming."

e. He explored the Hudson River

f. Boston patriot with big signature

g. He wrote the Declaration of Independence

h. She made the first flag

i. Governor of New Amsterdam

j. American naval commander in Revolution

k. Explorer who saved Jamestown colony and married an Indian princess

l. Navigator credited with discovering the New World

N.H. _____   W.B. _____   J.S. _____

H.H. _____   J.P.J. _____   J.H. _____

P.R. _____   W.P. _____   B.R. _____

T.J. _____   P.S. _____   C.C. _____

RANCH CHANCE

Yippee! Both cowboys have lassoed this steer. Or have they? What do you think? Try tracing the ropes to see who's the better cowboy.

WHAT'S THIS?

This picture was drawn by a European. It is supposed to be an American stagecoach of Revolutionary times. How many mistakes can you spot—including the big one?

MATCH THE WHITE HOUSE

Here, eleven matches (or toothpicks) make up the residence of our Presidents. Can you rearrange four of them so that eleven squares will appear?

SEVENTY-SIX

How can you turn seven matches into seventy-six?

CARPENTERS AND PRESIDENTS

What does one job have to do with the other? Fill in the missing letters and you'll find the answer to this riddle:

Why do carpenters believe there is no such thing as stone?

TAF＿

＿OOVER

KENN＿DY

T＿LER

GRA＿T

HAY＿S

ROOSE＿ELT

EIS＿NHOWER

T＿UMAN

JACK＿ON

H＿RDING

＿ILSON

P＿LK

JOH＿SON

MCKINL＿Y

LOVE CARPENTRY

PATCH THE WHITE HOUSE

The White House was burned by the British in 1814, but was soon rebuilt. Can you restore two original columns by fitting these pieces together? (Use arrows to show where the pieces should go or trace the shapes, cut them out, and put them together.)

WORD SHUFFLE

What do you get when I steps into the camera?

Fill in the names of seven animals by rearranging the words below, and the answer to the riddle will appear down the middle.

1. AND PA

2. O MUSE

3. HEROS (sandwiches)

4. H IRON (branding iron)

5. PIRAT(e)

6. C. MEAL (corn meal)

7. O CRAB

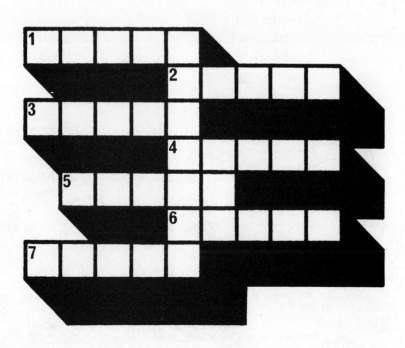

MONEY, MONEY

If you know your bills and coins, this puzzle will add up to real money for you. Instead of writing words, fill in the spaces with money, written as shown. When you've finished, the answers of your puzzle should add up to $78.47!

How to write it in the puzzle:

penny (common and rare)	01
nickel (common and rare)	05
dime	10
quarter	25
half dollar	50
1 dollar—bill or coin	100
5 dollar bill	500
10 dollar bill	1000
20 dollar bill	2000
50 dollar bill	5000

Across
1. Lincoln coin.
3. Washington bill.
5. Kennedy coin.
6. Eisenhower coin.
7. Washington coin.
9. Grant bill.
10. Buffalo (rare).

Down
1. Jefferson coin.
2. F. D. Roosevelt coin.
4. Indian copper (rare).
7. Jackson bill.
8. Same as 5 across.
9. Lincoln bill.

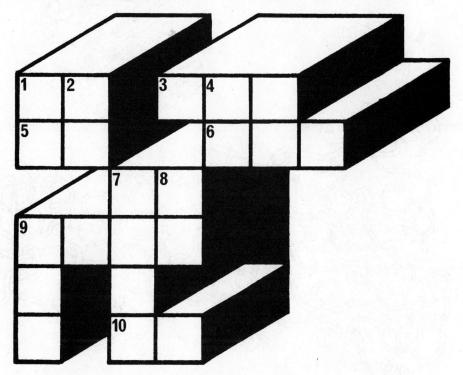

If Lincoln had owned a bill of Revolutionary money, what would you call it?
A Lincoln Continental.

How far will a silver dollar go today?
As far as you can throw it.

A LOFTY PROBLEM

In Revolutionary times there were no planes. But people did go aloft—in balloons. This balloon is still fastened to the ground, in spite of the man's panic, but by which rope?

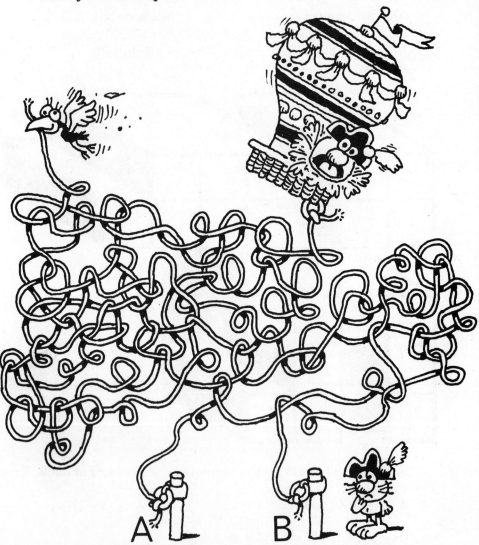

QUOTE ACROSTIC

If you can guess the words in these sentences, put them in the same-numbered boxes below, and you will have a famous saying by a Revolutionary patriot of Virginia.

1. Some of the patriots belonged to the Sons of _____.
2. "_____ the United Way."
3. The end for all living things.
4. _____, myself, and I.
5. He is to him as I is to _____.
6. It's either you _____ I.
7. "To _____ is better than to receive."

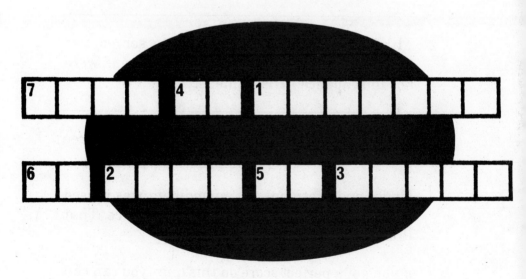

The speaker's name is P_____.

PRES. QUIZ

Among the twenty-four Presidents' names chosen for the word-find puzzle opposite are three names, each of which represents two different Presidents. Can you pick out the "twins" and give their full names?

1. _____

   _____

   _____

2. Although one of the men opposite served two terms, he was never re-elected. (His terms were not in sequence.) His name is:

   _____

3. One man was elected once, and re-elected three times. His full name is: _____

4. Under one President, an amendment was passed limiting a President to two terms in office. That President was: _____

5. If you got a perfect score on this quiz, you can run for President when you are _____ years of age, have lived in the U.S. _____ years, and IF you were born in the U.S. to start with.

PRESIDENTS WORD FIND

Can you find the names of twenty-four Presidents in the letter maze below? Here are the names to look for:

WASHINGTON	TAYLOR	WILSON
ADAMS	BUCHANAN	HARDING
MADISON	LINCOLN	HOOVER
MONROE	JOHNSON	TRUMAN
JACKSON	GRANT	IKE (Eisenhower)
VAN BUREN	CLEVELAND	KENNEDY
TYLER	ROOSEVELT	NIXON
POLK	TAFT	FORD

GREAT MOMENTS IN HISTORY
KITE FLYING

Here is our favorite man from history, Ben Franklin again, proving that lightning is electricity by flying his kite. But some of the things in this picture weren't around in Franklin's time. Can you name them?

INDIAN POWER MATCH

Draw a line from the Indian group or chief to the facts that fit.

SEMINOLES

1. Cherokee leader who developed first written Indian alphabet.

CHIEF
JOSEPH

2. Connecticut Indians who, led by Uncas, helped colonists against British.

NAVAHO

3. Indians living in Florida swamps who sheltered runaway slaves.

SITTING
BULL

4. Sheep-herding Indians skilled in weaving and metalwork.

MOHEGANS

5. Once powerful Eastern tribes. Men now often work on bridges and high buildings.

SEQUOYA

6. Leader of Nez Percé tribe who fought for lands in Oregon.

CHEROKEE
NATION

7. Famous Sioux chief who led Indians against Custer at Battle of Little Big Horn.

IROQUOIS

8. Indian farmers with houses, schools, etc. in Georgia, forced to march to Oklahoma ("Trail of Tears").

CITY SENSE

What city's name commemorates the greatest feat of strength ever performed in the U.S.?

Wheeling, West Virginia

Why is our national capital such a clean city?

Because it's "Washington, Washington," Monday through Sunday.

What would you do if you found Chicago, Ill?

Get a Baltimore, M.D.

What did Nashville, Tennessee?

Exactly what Little Rock, Arkansas.

GIVE THEM BACK THE USA

The words below need the letters U, S, and A to give them meaning. Can you supply these important letters in the right places?

1. P _ _ _ E
2. _ M _ _ E
3. _ Q _ _ B B L E
4. _ _ _ _ G E
5. Q _ _ R T _
6. C _ _ _ E
7. _ Q _ _ D

8. _ _ G _ R
9. _ _ U _ L
10. G _ _ R D _
11. S Q _ _ _ H
12. _ _ _ C Y
13. N A _ _ E _
14. L _ _ G H _

BIG SQUARE DANCE CROSSWORD

Across

1. To exchange.
5. Play a _____ (song).
9. Graceful whirling dance for partners.
11. ___ what? (slang).
12. Kitchen Patrol (abbrev.).
14. Present tense of was.
15. Rhoda's mother's name on TV.
16. Square dance step; rhymes with glide.
19. _____ hands (noise).
20. Opposite of bad.
22. Opposite of work.
24. Second word in 2 down.
27. Wisconsin (old abbrev.).
28. "They danced by the light of the _____."
29. Move to and fro.
31. Medical (abbrev.).
32. United Nations (abbrev.).
34. Missouri (abbrev.).
35. Virginia _____ (square dance).
36. Place for storing wood or tools.
37. Yell of pain.

Down

1. "_____ _____ partner"; (square dance call).
2. "T_____ the night before Christmas . . ."
3. Short for Albert.
4. Barnum's first 2 initials.
6. Initials of our country.
7. Opposite of yes.
8. "_____ ___ ___ Lou" (square dance tune).
10. "Old _____ Coon" (square dance tune).
13. Paid (abbrev.).
16. Crafty.
17. Louisiana (abbrev.).
18. "_____ to your partner."
19. California (abbrev.).
21. Motion of 18 down.
23. Opposite of high.
25. _____ down; square dance event.
26. To finish.
29. Same as 11 across.
30. What's left after a fire.
33. Northeast (abbrev.).

Answers

p. 12 STAR ATHLETES

Ice-Skating Stars: Rosalynn Sumners,Elaine Zayak,Dorothy Hamill
Tennis Stars: Bjorn Borg, Martina Navratilova
Basketball Stars: Kareem Abdul Jabbar, Larry Bird
Football Stars: Joe Namath, Joe Green, Roger Staubach
Track Stars: Mary Decker, Evelyn Ashford
Swimming Star: Mark Spitz
Golf Stars: Lee Trevino, Nancy Lopez
Baseball Stars: Babe Ruth, Yogi Berra
Gymnastics Stars: Nadia Comaneci, Olga Korbut
Hockey Stars: Bob Nystrom, Bobby Orr, Wayne Gretzky
Boxing Stars: Muhammad Ali, Joe Frazier
Auto Racing Stars: A.J. Foyt, Al Unser, Mario Andretti

p. 3   *Explosive Crossword:* Pop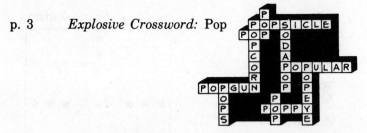

p. 4   *Big Day:* Gr<u>ind</u>ers; r<u>epe</u>llent; blu<u>nder</u>buss; com-
       me<u>nce</u>ment; holi<u>day</u>.

p. 5   *Magic Squares:*
       Uncle Sam; Eagle

p. 6   *Moving the Sentries:* Nickel from A to F; dime
       from C to B, B to A; nickel from E to B, B to C,
       from F to E, E to B; dime from D to E; nickel
       from B to D.

p. 7   *Pick Your Colors:* 1. blue; 2. red; 3. white; 4. red;
       5. red; 6. red; 7. blue; 8. red; 9. red; 10. blue;
       11. white; 12. blue; 13. red; 14. red; 15. red;
       16. red; 17. blue; 18. white; 19. red; 20. white;
       21. red; 22. blue; 23. white; 24. red.

p. 8   *Words from the White House:* the, it, out, he, use,
       U.S., St., I.O.U., these, see, tee, wee, hew, tout,
       wet, west, twit, sheet, sew, to, wit, whet, whee,
       stew, we, us, set, suit, sue, oust, she, suet, with.

p. 9   *Discovery Acrostic:* Wipe; help; knot;
       last; lessen. He went to see.

p. 10 *Seat a Treasured Man:* Hamilton

p. 11 *Presidential Patter:* 1. Garfield,
       Cleveland 2. Grant 3. Pierce
       4. Polk 5. Fillmore 6. Coolidge
       7. Lincoln 8. All were sons; six
       show it in their names.

p. 13   *Pet Hate Crossword:*
George the Third

p. 14   *Star Divider:*

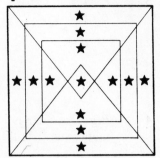

p. 15   *Ladies' Match:* 1. Dolly Madison 2. Jacqueline Kennedy 3. Eleanor Roosevelt 4. Martha Washington 5. Mary Lincoln 6. Abigail Adams

p. 17   *Famous Firsts:* 1. Two terms in office 2. William H. Taft 3. James Buchanan 4. Theodore Roosevelt 5. John Adams 6. Richard M. Nixon 7. Dolly Madison

p. 18   *Constitutional:* 1. picnic 2. soon 3. knit 4. paste 5. stub 6. bite 7. stir 8. mute 9. catsup 10. pinch 11. cool 12. once

p. 21   *Presidents in Hiding:* 1. with a 'yes' 2. attic level and 3. a dam straight 4. style reading 5. hangar fields 6. poncho over 7. "Get after 8. John so nosy 9. That Rumanian 10. afford 11. dog ran to 12. Interpol knew 13. mad is on.

p. 22   *Famous Monograms:* John Hancock, Gerald Ford

p. 23   *Birds of America Word Find:*

p. 24   *Target Practice:* 3, 6, 9, 11, 14, 15

p. 25   *Mystery Letters Puzzle:*
US

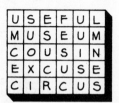

p. 26-27 *Monster Number:*

p. 28   *Switches:* Texas — Taxes; United — Untied; Lincoln — Conn./Ill.; Males — Salem.

p. 29   *Fireworks for the Fourth:*

FIRE   FOUR
FORE   POUR
FORK   POOR
WORK   POOL
           POLL
           PULL
           DULL
           DULY
           JULY

p. 30-31 *Mystery Man of History:*

p. 32   *Big Tea Party:* Patriots 3 and 4

p. 33   *Put the TEA Back!* 1. steam   2. treat   3. seats 4. waiter   5. late   6. tame   7. east   8. beast   9. tread 10. death   11. plate   12. meat   13. stare   14. paste 15. metal 16. stake

p. 34   *Clothing States:* If Florida and Virginia con Louise E. Ana for the coat of Miss Ouri, will Dela wear new jersey? I don't know. I'll ask her. Did Minnie sew the new jersey for me? If so, I owe her.
Ken Tucky, did you sew the coat of Missus Ippi? No, the coat of Georgia. Ah can saw, too.

p. 35   *Mystery Landmark:* Valley Forge

p. 36   *Military Maze:* 10 - 12 - 30 - 8 - 15 - 25; Garrison D.

p. 37   *Who Said It?* 1. Lincoln 2. T. Roosevelt 3. Wilson 4. Hoover 5. F.D. Roosevelt 6. Truman 7. Kennedy

p. 38   *Secret Word:* P O A T A S I A B E I W
         I N D E P E N D E N C E
         E E E A E N D E D E E

p. 39   *Famous Initials Match:* NH (Nathan Hale) — c.; HH (Henry Hudson) — e.; PR (Paul Revere) — d.; TJ (Thomas Jefferson) — g; WB (William Bradford) — a.; JPJ (John Paul Jones) — j; WP (William Penn) — b; PS (Peter Stuyvesant) — i; JS (John Smith) — k; JH (John Hancock) — f; BR (Betsy Ross) — h; CC (Christopher Columbus) — l.

p. 40   *Ranch Chance:* Cowboy number 2

p. 41   *What's This?* 1. First of all, it isn't a stagecoach, but a covered wagon! 2. It's being driven out West, which wasn't explored until after 1800. 3. Driver is wearing western clothes. 4. There's a Paris, Maine, but "3 kilometers" sign indicates Paris, France. 5. Lantern is lit although sun is shining. 6. Rubber tire on wheel was not invented then. 7. American flag didn't have so many stars at that time. 8. Coachman's whip is a fishing rod and reel. 9. There's a plane in the sky! 10. There's a saddle on the horse. 11. Pipe is upside down.

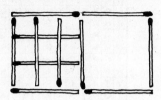 
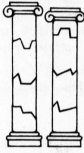 
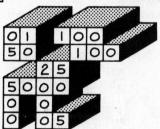

p. 51   *Presidents Word Find:*

p. 52   *Great Moments in History*: *Kite Flying:* Franklin's friend is wearing modern clothes and a wrist watch, and carries a portable radio. Franklin is wearing galoshes. Other mistakes: TV aerials; hydrant; skyscrapers; electric billboards, street light, traffic light; telephone booth; motorcycle; bus; truck; cars; plane; helicopter; elevated train.

p. 53   *Indian Power Match:* Seminoles-3; Chief Joseph-6; Navaho-4; Sitting Bull-7; Mohegans-2; Sequoya-1; Cherokee Nation-8; Iroquois-5.

p. 55   *Give Them Back the USA:* 1. pause 2. amuse 3. squabble 4. usage 5. quarts 6. cause 7. squad 8. sugar 9. usual 10. guards 11. squash 12. saucy 13. nausea 14. laughs

p. 57   *Big Square Dance Crossword:*